The Japanese

The Japanese

Pamela Odijk

Silver Burdett Press

Acknowledgments

The author and publishers are grateful to the following for permission to reproduce copyright photographs and prints:

ANT: (M.F. Soper) pp. 12, 31, 33, (Silvestris) p. 13 left, (Otto Rogge) pp. 13 right, 26, 34; International Society for Educational Information, Tokyo, Inc. pp. 9, 27; Ronald Sheridan/The Ancient Art and Architecture Collection: cover, pp. 10, 14, 21, 22, 23, 24, 28, 36, 39; Werner Forman Archive pp. 15, 16, 17, 18, 19, 25, 29, 32, 35, 37, 38, 40, 42.

While every care has been taken to trace and acknowledge copyright, the publishers tender their apologies for any accidental infringement where copyright has proved untraceable. They would be pleased to come to a suitable arrangement with the rightful owner in each case.

First published 1989 by
THE MACMILLAN COMPANY OF AUSTRALIA PTY LTD
107 Moray Street, South Melbourne 3205
6 Clarke Street, Crows Nest 2065

Adapted and first published in the United States in 1991
by Silver Burdett Press, Englewood Cliffs, N.J.

Library of Congress Cataloging-in-Publication Data

Odijk, Pamela.
   The Japanese / Pamela Odijk.
      p.   cm—(The Ancient world)
   Includes index.
   Summary: Surveys the history of old Japan and describes its life
and culture before the country was opened up to the West.
   1. Japan—Juvenile literature. [1. Japan—Civilization.]
I. Title. II. Series: Odijk, Pamela   Ancient world.
DS806.047   1991
952—dc20   91-13796
   ISBN 0-382-09898-6 (lib. bdg.)   CIP
   ISBN 0-382-24272-6 (pbk.)   AC

Printed in Hong Kong

The Japanese

Contents

The Japanese: Timeline

Prehistoric.
Jomon Culture arose in Japan around 8000 B.C. The origin of the Jomon people is unknown. They had a hunting and gathering culture, used stone and bone tools, and made pottery with distinctive designs. Around 300 B.C. the Jomon Culture began to be displaced by the Yayoi Culture, imported by migrants from Manchuria and Korea. The Yayoi people introduced rice farming, horses, weaving, and wheel-made pottery. Eventually the Jomon people were absorbed, exterminated, or displaced by the Yayoi people.

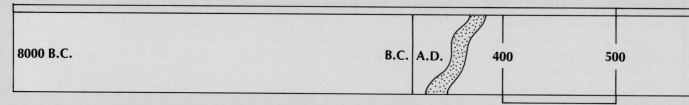

| 8000 B.C. | | B.C. | A.D. | 400 | 500 |

A powerful clan in the Yamato region, near Nara, began expanding its domain around A.D. 400. The Yamato rulers took the title of "emperor" and claimed to be of divine origin, directly descended from the sun goddess. Buddhism was introduced to Japan from Korea around A.D. 551.

Kamakura period.
Yoritomo becomes Japan's first shogun, and establishes military capital at Kamakura. Mongols under Kublai Khan make two attempts to invade Japan.

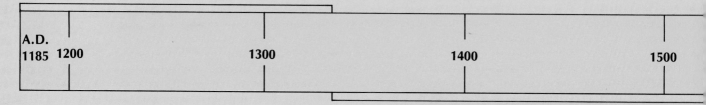

| A.D. 1185 | 1200 | 1300 | 1400 | 1500 |

Muromachi (Ashikaga) period.
Military government returns to Kyoto, which becomes a great cultural center again. Rise of Zen, with influence in art, Noh theater, tea ceremony, and literature. Trade with China; rise of commerce and manufacturing. Period ends in civil war.

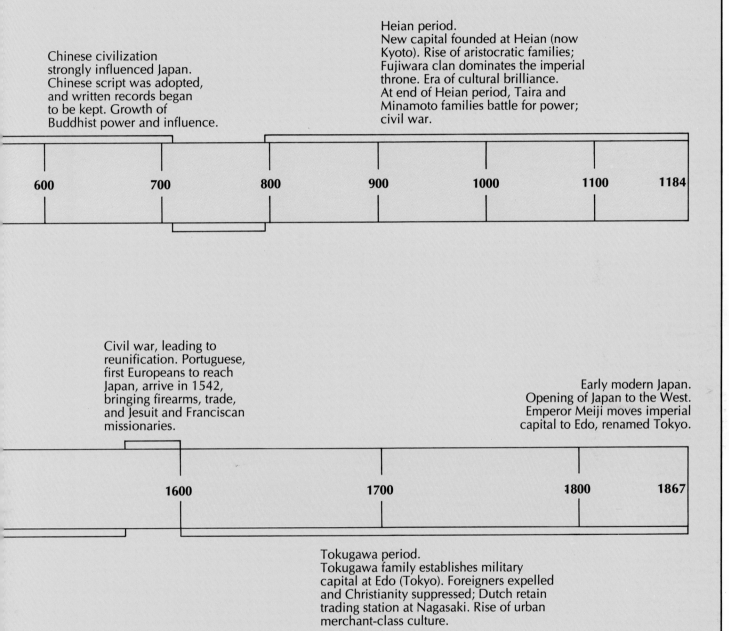

Chinese civilization
strongly influenced Japan.
Chinese script was adopted,
and written records began
to be kept. Growth of
Buddhist power and influence.

Heian period.
New capital founded at Heian (now
Kyoto). Rise of aristocratic families;
Fujiwara clan dominates the imperial
throne. Era of cultural brilliance.
At end of Heian period, Taira and
Minamoto families battle for power;
civil war.

600   700   800   900   1000   1100   1184

Civil war, leading to
reunification. Portuguese,
first Europeans to reach
Japan, arrive in 1542,
bringing firearms, trade,
and Jesuit and Franciscan
missionaries.

Early modern Japan.
Opening of Japan to the West.
Emperor Meiji moves imperial
capital to Edo, renamed Tokyo.

1600   1700   1800   1867

Tokugawa period.
Tokugawa family establishes military
capital at Edo (Tokyo). Foreigners expelled
and Christianity suppressed; Dutch retain
trading station at Nagasaki. Rise of urban
merchant-class culture.

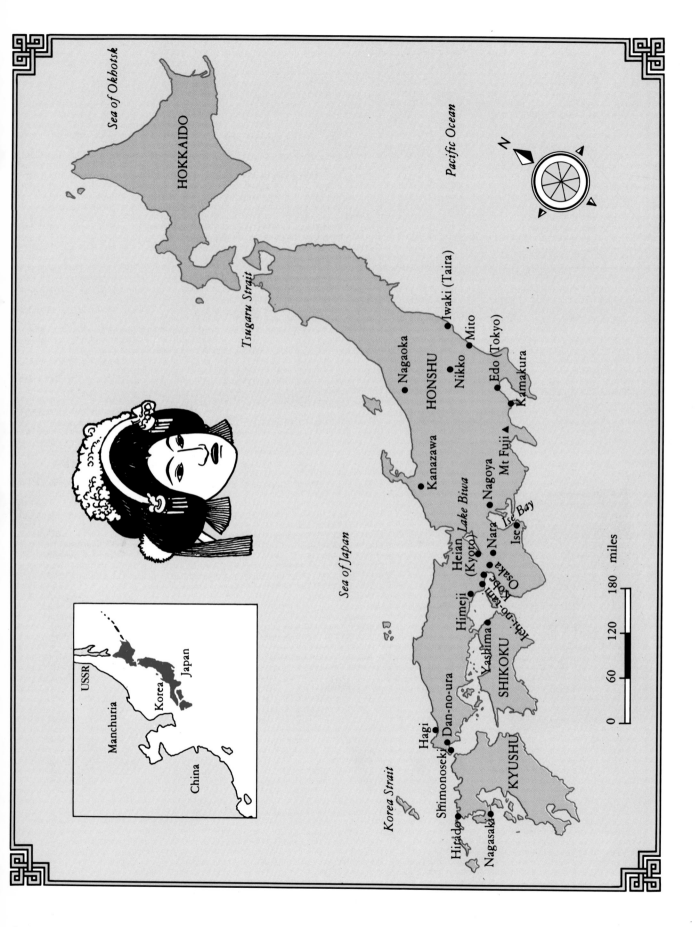

Sea of Okhotsk

HOKKAIDO

Tsugaru Strait

Pacific Ocean

N

Iwaki (Taira)

Mito

Nagaoka

Nikko

HONSHU

Edo (Tokyo)

Kamakura

Kanazawa

Mt Fuji ▲

Nagoya

Lake Biwa

Ise Bay

Sea of Japan

Heian (Kyoto)

Nara

Ise

Osaka

Kobe

Himeji

Ichi-no-tani

Yashima

SHIKOKU

Dan-no-ura

Hagi

Shimonoseki

KYUSHU

Hirado

Nagasaki

Korea Strait

USSR

Manchuria

Korea

Japan

China

0   60   120   180   miles

The Japanese: Introduction

Before the Chinese writing system was introduced into Japan in the fifth century A.D., the Japanese had no written historical records. What we know about Japan's history before this time comes from Japanese legends and folklore, and the work of **anthropologists** and **archaeologists.** From these sources, the early history of Japan is gradually being pieced together.

The earliest known inhabitants of Japan were the people of the Jomon Culture, who lived in isolation from the rest of the world for about 10,000 years. The Jomon people were displaced by later arrivals, the ancestors of the present-day Japanese. Most of these new people came from northeastern Asia, and arrived from the mainland by way of Korea around 2,300 years ago.

Japanese painting of a Franciscan monk. The Franciscan monks arrived in Japan during the period of unification, A.D. 1573-1600.

At around the same time, smaller groups of migrants came to Japan via Taiwan and Okinawa. These people probably intermarried with each other as well as with the original inhabitants of the islands. The Ainu people of Hokkaido, Japan's northernmost main island, may be descended from some of Japan's original inhabitants.

The new migrants to Japan created a new culture, called the Yayoi Culture. The Yayoi people cultivated rice, rode horses, used bronze weapons and ornaments, and made pottery using a potter's wheel. At first they were organized into many small kingdoms, ruled by a warrior class. Kings were buried in huge, elaborate tombs after they died.

By around A.D. 500, the rulers of the kingdom of Yamato (near present-day Kyoto, Nara, and Osaka) claimed the right to rule all of Japan. They adopted the Chinese-style title **emperor** *(tenno),* and claimed that their mythical first ancestor, Emperor Jimmu, was descended from the Sun Goddess. Gradually,

Japanese woodblock print of Mt. Fuji, the highest mountain in Japan.

other territorial rulers became a **feudal** aristocracy. Ordinary peasants, **artisans,** and merchants were under the complete control of the aristocracy.

The religion of the Yayoi people was a kind of nature-worship called *Shinto,* "the way of the gods." In A.D. 551, Buddhism was introduced from China via Korea, and soon became established in Japan.

In A.D. 710, Japan's first permanent capital city was established at Nara. Soon the capital was moved, first to Nagaoka in 784 and then to Heian-kyo (later called Kyoto) in 794. Heian-kyo remained Japan's imperial capital for over 1,000 years. The emperor and the high aristocracy led lives of luxury in Heian-kyo for several hundred years. The emperors theoretically were absolute rulers, but often they had very little real power. During most of the Heian period (794-1185), the emperors were puppets of the head of the powerful Fujiwara clan.

In the twelfth century A.D., civil war broke out between the Taira and Minamoto clans, powerful provincial military aristocrats. The Minamoto won, and established a new military capital at Kamakura. Thereafter, Japan always had a military ruler, called a **shogun,** who exercised real power; the emperors remained on the throne, but were powerless. The old court aristocracy died out, and a new ruling class of **daimyo** (military lords) and **samurai** (warriors) arose.

The last family of shoguns, the Tokugawa, came to power in 1600. They attempted to close off Japan completely from the outside world, though some European missionaries had already reached Japan, and a few Dutch merchants were allowed to conduct trade there. From about 1850, however, there was increased contact with Western peoples, and this contact, over time, brought tremendous changes to Japan.

Japan's history can be divided into the following periods:

Date	Name of Period	Some Important Events
8000 B.C. to A.D. 500	Prehistoric	Jomon Culture. The Jomon people had a hunting and gathering culture. They used stone and bone tools, and made pottery which had distinctive designs. Around 300 B.C. the Jomon Culture was displaced by the Yayoi Culture, developed by migrants from mainland Asia. The Yayoi introduced rice farming, weaving, bronze, and wheel-made pottery. Small kingdoms ruled by a military aristocracy developed, leading to the unification of Japan under the emperors of the Yamato Kingdom.
Classical Period A.D. 500-710	Early historic	Influence of Chinese civilization, via Korea. The Japanese adopted the written Chinese language and began to keep records. Buddhism was introduced in 551; Buddhist temples founded around 600 by Prince Shotoku.
A.D. 710-794	Nara period	Nara, the first permanent capital, was founded in A.D. 710. Chinese cultural influence continues. Buddhist temples become powerful.
A.D. 794-1185	Heian period	New capital founded at Heian-kyo (Kyoto). Brilliant era of aristocratic culture. Period ends with civil war of Taira and Minamoto clans.
Shogunate A.D. 1185-1333	Kamakura period	Minamoto Yoritomo becomes first shogun, starting period of military rule. Rise of samurai (warrior) class. Mongol invasions defeated.
A.D. 1333-1573	Ashikaga period	Shogunal capital returns to Kyoto. Rise of Zen Buddhism, with artistic influence in Noh theater and ink painting. Trade with China. Rise of commerce and industry. Period ends in civil war.
1573-1600	Period of unification	Civil war. First Europeans arrive, 1542. Firearms introduced. Jesuit and Franciscan missionaries. Country unified by Tokugawa clan.
1600-1867	Tokugawa period	Arts flourish; architecture, gardens, tea ceremony reach new heights. Rise of urban culture, Kabuki theater, woodblock prints. Country closed to most foreigners.
Modern Japan Nineteenth century	Early modern Japan	Influence of Western learning via Dutch merchants. Japan forcibly opened to foreign trade by Commodore Perry in 1853.

The Importance of Landforms and Climate

Japan is made up of a chain of 4,223 **volcanic islands.** The four largest islands—Hokkaido, Honshu, Shikoku, and Kyushu—make up about 98 percent of Japan's total land area. The Japanese archipelago is situated off the coast of the USSR, Korea, and China, separated by the Sea of Japan. The Pacific Ocean is off the east coast of Japan. Most of the land is mountainous which makes agriculture difficult. Only 16 percent of Japan's land is arable: this land is found in the short and narrow river valleys and on small plains. The slopes of some hills and mountains have been terraced in order to increase the amount of land suitable for agriculture. Most of the rivers in Japan are short and fast flowing.

The highest mountain is Mt. Fuji which rises to 12,388 feet (3,776 meters). Japan's mountainous landscape has many volcanoes, some of which are active. Japan has many active seismic faults, which produce frequent earth tremors and occasional severe earthquakes.

Conifer forests on Hokkaido Island. In the background rise mountain peaks which are common throughout the Japanese landscape. Some mountains are live volcanoes.

The Japanese adapted their lifestyle and architecture to withstand this threat.

Soils

The most fertile soils in Japan can be found on the coastal lowlands. The volcanic soils of the mountainous areas are thin and not suitable for crop cultivation.

Climate

Japan has a temperate climate with four seasons, though the climate varies from north to south. In the north the winters are long, cold, and snowy, while the summers are short and cool. Moving south, the winters become shorter and milder, and the summers longer and hot.

During the winter, cold dry winds blow from the Asian mainland to Japan. The winds pick up moisture from the Japan Sea and deposit heavy snowfalls on the northwestern coast. During the summer, moist warm winds blow from the Pacific, bringing plenty of rain. Japan is affected by summer typhoons that often cause much devastation.

Natural Plants, Animals, and Birds

Because of the climatic conditions and the abundance of running water, Japan's plains and highlands are covered with thick vegetation. Evergreen forest trees, native camphor and cypress grow in the north while the warmer south has blossoming cherries, maples, and other ornamental trees. Wood from the forests together with bamboo are used for building, and to make practical utensils and ornaments.

In the high mountain areas, all vegetation gives way to stunted trees and treeless plains.

Japan's land mammals are of species similar to those of the nearby Asian mainland. Bears, wild boars, badgers, foxes, deer, and monkeys, including the Japanese **macaque,** are native to Japan. In the high mountain areas live antelopes, hares, and weasels.

Japan's native birds include gulls, auks, grebes, albatrosses, shearwaters, heron,

Above: autumn colors of Kyoto, Honshu.

Left: Macaque adult with baby. Macaques are native to Japan. Their thick furry coat enables them to survive in below zero temperatures.

storks, ibis, ducks, geese, swans and cranes. Cormorants are also native to Japan. Sometimes they are domesticated and used to catch fish. Japan also has over one hundred and fifty species of songbirds. Other birds include hawks, falcons, pheasants, quail, owls, woodpeckers, and ptarmigan.

The Sea of Japan supports a large variety of sea life, including whales, dolphins, salmon, sardines, sea bream, mackerel, tuna, trout, herring, and cod. Crabs, shrimps, prawns, and oysters are also found along the shores.

Japan also supports a variety of reptilian life, including snakes (most of which are harmless), turtles, tortoises, sea snakes, lizards, frogs, and giant salamanders which can grow up to 5 feet (1.5 meters) long.

Crops, Herds, and Hunting

Crops

In ancient times in Japan, the population was small and much vacant land was available. Members of the ruling class extended their power by recruiting peasants to bring new land under cultivation. But by the end of the Heian Period (twelfth century A.D.), the population had grown and farm land became relatively scarce. Japanese farmers began to practice intensive agriculture, designed to produce the highest possible crop yield from the land.

Rice was, and still is, the main crop grown by Japanese farmers. Rice is grown in small, terraced paddy fields to regulate the supply of water during the growing cycle.

Rice, the principal crop, was grown in **paddy fields,** which had to be terraced, leveled, and provided with elaborate irrigation systems. Larger fields were plowed with oxen, while smaller ones were worked with hoes and other hand tools. Manure, ashes, and compost were used as fertilizer. In the harvest season, the rice was cut and threshed by hand.

In addition to rice, grain crops included wheat, buckwheat, millet, and barley. Vegetables and soybeans were also cultivated, along with fruit trees, mulberry trees, and tea bushes.

Because of Japan's wet climate, in the fields peasants wore rain capes, called *mino*, made of straw. They also wore broad cone-shaped hats to protect them from both rain and sun.

Rice Field Ritual

In order to ensure a good harvest, peasants performed a ritual called *tasobi* before planting their fields. Drummers led the peasants in performing songs and dances in the fields, in order to win the favor of the *kami* (gods or spirits). Offerings were made to the local gods at small shrines that were built in front of sacred trees, rocks, and springs near the fields.

Herds and Hunting

Japan lacked wide expanses of grassland upon which to graze animals. There were few domestic animals: draft oxen and an occasional pack horse, as well as chickens. Horses were also raised for military use. Both Shinto and Buddhism discouraged unnecessary killing and the eating of meat. Blood, hides, and other animal products were regarded as unclean. Therefore the Japanese were generally not hunters, though small birds were caught in nets for food, and members of the samurai (warrior) class sometimes hunted wild boar for sport.

The sea provided the Japanese with an abundant supply of fish and shellfish, which added protein to their diet. Seaweed was also collected for food.

A Japanese Feudal Estate

Some Japanese peasants were independent small landowners, but for most of Japanese history, most farmers were tenants of large estates. Depending on the historical period, the estate owner might be a member of the old civil aristocracy, a Buddhist temple, or a member of the military aristocracy. Low-ranking members of the samurai class were farmer-warriors who worked land granted to them by their feudal lords, while ordinary peasants worked land belonging to others, and had to pay rent to the landlord.

Large landowners often lived in grand houses far from their estates. Local agents or **bailiffs** were responsible for managing the fields and collecting rent. Peasants typically had to pay sixty percent of their crops as rent.

Japanese feudal lord's villa in Yokohama.

How Families Lived

The family was the basic unit of Japanese society, and everything centered around it. For most people, the family meant essentially a small three-generation household. Members of the upper classes relied on more extended family relationships to protect and exercise their positions of power in society. However, within the samurai military class, ties of feudal loyalty sometimes conflicted with family obligations; a warrior's duties to his feudal lord took precedence over those to his own family.

Ideally, a family would be headed by an adult male in the prime of life. Elderly men retired from positions of active leadership, though they were shown great respect and their advice was often heeded. The head of a family had absolute authority within his household, and all other members of the family had to submit to his will.

Women were expected to follow the "three obediences": to father, husband, and son. In ancient times, women could own and inherit

Detail from an early seventeenth century screen depicting Nijo Castle, home of the Tokugawa family in Kyoto.

property, but that right was withdrawn after the end of the Heian period. Marriages were arranged by the parents of the bride and groom, who were given no choice in the matter. Ordinary men had one wife, but wealthy men often kept **concubines** in addition to their official wife.

Houses of the Wealthy

In the Nara and Heian periods, members of the aristocracy lived in large urban palaces of Chinese-style architecture. Such houses usually had three wings enclosing a garden, and had wooden walls, heavy tile roofs, and polished wooden floors.

In later times, such palaces were replaced by a new style of architecture that had many distinctively Japanese features. Floors were covered with heavy mats, called *tatami*, woven from rice straw. Interior walls were often made from sliding wooden panels covered with heavy paper. Other sliding panels, called *shoji*, were covered in thin, translucent paper, and served as windows or as doors.

Such houses had very little furniture. People sat on flat pillows, and used low tables for dining or as desks. Special alcoves were built into some walls, for the display of scroll paintings and art objects. Clothing was stored in wooden chests. Sleeping mats were rolled up and put away in cupboards during the day, and unrolled for use at night. Houses were heated with portable charcoal **braziers.** Shoes were not worn indoors, in order not to damage the tatami mat floors.

Daimyo, the highest-ranking members of the samurai class, lived in large castles surrounded by walls and moats, while ordinary samurai lived in fortified farmhouses. During the Tokugawa period, daimyo were also required to maintain houses in the shogunal capital at Edo. These houses, like the houses of wealthy urban merchants, often had two stories and were built behind a wall facing the street.

Houses of Poorer Families

Poorer homes in cities and towns were similar in design to those of the wealthy, but were

Sixteenth century screen depicting a swordsmith at work in his workshop.

smaller and lacked courtyards and gardens. Farmhouses were dark and cramped, and were organized around a central hearth from which smoke escaped through a vent in the roof.

Merchants and Artisans

In cities, many people engaged in trade, or in manufacturing goods such as textiles, swords and armor, ceramics, and lacquerwork. Merchants and artisans ranged from the very wealthy to the very poor.

Education

In the Nara and Heian periods, education was limited to the sons of wealthy families and to Buddhist priests and monks. Later, with the growth of cities, education became more widespread. By 1850, Japan had one of the highest literacy rates in the world.

Food and Medicine

Rice was (and still is) the staple food of Japan, eaten at every meal along with fish, fresh or pickled vegetables, seaweed, and other side dishes. Noodles made of wheat or buckwheat also were an important source of carbohydrates in the diet. The diet of poor people depended heavily on rice and noodles, while richer people could afford a larger amount and variety of other dishes. Fish was eaten raw, broiled, boiled, or salted. Soybean cakes *(tofu)* also were an important source of protein. Buddhism discouraged the eating of red meat, but chicken, duck, and wildfowl were often eaten. Soups containing noodles, vegetables, seafood, and eggs were also popular.

The Japanese placed great stress on the importance of fine cooking and of serving food in an attractive manner. Upper class households were equipped with a large variety of beautiful plates and serving utensils of pottery, porcelain, lacquerware, and bamboo. The etiquette of eating was also important, and good table manners were seen as a mark of a refined person.

Food was served on trays containing individual bowls of rice along with side dishes arranged on small plates and bowls. People knelt or sat cross-legged on mats while eating. Food was eaten with chopsticks made of wood, bamboo, bone, or ivory. Food was often accompanied by heated rice wine **(sake),** drunk from tiny ceramic cups. Tea was served at the beginning and the end of the meal.

Sweets were not usually served at meals, but rather were eaten as snacks. Tiny cakes made from rice flour and sugar were fashioned into delicate shapes of flowers and leaves and were served on special occasions, such as weddings and festivals.

Tea Ceremony (Cha-no-yu)

Tea was brought to Japan from China by Buddhist monks during the Heian period. Ordinary tea was drunk as a simple beverage, but in Zen monasteries a special tea-drinking ceremony also evolved and became popular from the Ashikaga period onwards. For the tea ceremony, which developed into an elaborate ritual with many rules of etiquette, a particular kind of powdered green tea was served in beautiful drinking bowls. Members of the upper classes had special tea rooms in their houses, or tea pavilions in their gardens, reserved for the tea ceremony.

Left: Eighteenth century drinking bowl with image of Mt Fuji, used in the tea ceremony.

Opposite: Part of the main building of the Katsura Imperial Villa in Kyoto. The gardens were laid out in the early seventeenth century. The interior was designed to appear to merge into the garden. This building was known as Pine Lute Pavilion because of the sound of the wind in the trees.

The Tea Ceremony Rituals

Before entering the tea room, guests were required to scoop water with a bamboo dipper, and wash their hands and mouths.

The signal to enter the tea pavilion was given by the sound of wooden clappers.

When everyone was seated, the water for the tea was heated in a two handled urn made of iron. Extra charcoal for the stove was kept nearby in a wicker basket.

Powdered green tea was taken from a special lacquered container and placed in a small bowl.

The tea master scooped the hot water with a wooden dipper and poured it over the tea.

The mixture was then beaten to a froth with a bamboo whisk called a *chasen*.

The tea bowl was then passed to the first guest.

Each guest took exactly three sips, cleaned the rim of the bowl, and passed it to the next guest.

When the bowl was emptied it would be passed around again and examined as a work of art.

No trivial gossip was to be indulged in and no flattery was permitted.

No ceremony was to last beyond four hours.

Medicine

In ancient times, the Japanese used some medicines made from herbs and animal products, but the treatment of disease also depended heavily on magic and religious rituals. Prayers, chants, and other techniques were used to drive away evil spirits that were thought to cause disease.

During the Nara and Heian periods, Chinese-style medicine was brought to Japan by Buddhist monks, making available a wider range of medical treatments. A diagnosis was made through careful physical examination of the patient, with special attention to the pulse. Herbal remedies, designed to balance hot and cold energies within the body, were pre-scribed. Acupuncture, which involved the insertion of thin needles into the skin at selected points on the body, was used to treat some illnesses, and massage was also used as a medical therapy.

Doctors were trained by serving as assistants to practicing doctors. Textbooks and encyclopedias of herbal remedies, often based on Chinese works, were also available for medical education.

European-style medical theory and practice was introduced to Japan by the Dutch during the seventeenth and eighteenth centuries. This was of only limited usefulness, because European medicine was not highly advanced at the time, but it did lead to some improvements in the practice of surgery.

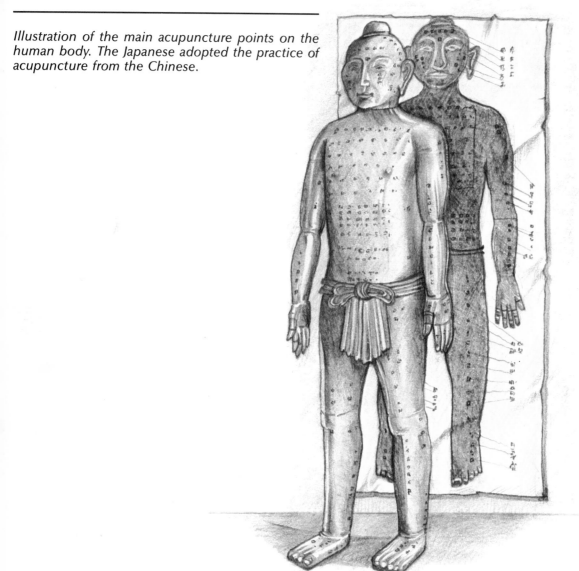

Illustration of the main acupuncture points on the human body. The Japanese adopted the practice of acupuncture from the Chinese.

Clothes

Working-class people in Japan wore clothing made of hemp, linen, or cotton, while silk clothing was worn by the wealthy. The style of Japanese clothing went through a number of dramatic changes over time; the kimono that is now thought of as the "typical" Japanese costume was a relatively late development.

Clothing in ancient times, known from clay figurines dating from the third to fifth cen-

Seventeenth century pottery figure of a woman in traditional dress. Around the neckline can be seen the layered effect of wearing different colored garments.

Nineteenth century woodblock print showing a samurai dressed in the black cap and formal robes of a court official attended by two servants.

turies A.D., consisted of a two-piece costume for both men and women. The upper garment was a jacket that flared out over the hips. For men, this was worn over wide trousers, while women wore pleated skirts. This type of costume continued to be worn during the seventh to eighth centuries.

During the Nara period, in the eighth century, Japan began to be strongly influenced by Chinese culture, and the clothing of the upper classes began to reflect contemporary Chinese styles. For riding and other outdoor activities, men wore black trousers and silk tunics, covered by a flowing silk robe that often was very brightly colored. Indoors, for informal wear, they wore long robes closed with a sash.

During the Nara and Heian periods, women's dress became extremely elaborate, and women of the aristocracy paid a great deal of attention to dressing fashionably. A woman's costume consisted of loose silk trousers, over

which were worn several silk robes of different colors, one on top of the other. These robes were arranged so that the layers were visible at the hem, sleeves, and neckline, producing a rainbow color effect.

Complicated rules governed the number of layers of robes that could be worn by aristocratic women, and their colors, so that the rank and status of a person could be seen from her dress. Similar rules applied to the clothing of men. The emperor, the empress, and the highest officials of the imperial court wore the most elaborate clothing, including special garments that were used only for certain ceremonies and rituals.

During the Kamakura period (twelfth century), with the rise of the samurai military class and the decline of the old Heian aristocracy, upper-class clothing became somewhat simpler, though it was still very colorful and costly. Women of the samurai class wore fewer layers of robes, and were expected to dress modestly outside the home. When they left their houses, they wore large, plain outer robes and large hats from which a veil was draped, concealing their faces. For men, the old Heian trousers and tunic developed into a new costume worn for formal occasions. This consisted of a robe worn as an undergarment, a stiff jacket that flared widely at the shoulders and hips, and wide, flat trousers.

The Kimono

During the Ashikaga period (fourteenth to fifteenth centuries), the kimono—a long, flowing robe worn with a sash—became the standard garment for both men and women. Although the garment itself was cut in a simple style, advances in weaving and dyeing techniques made it possible to produce kimonos of exceptional beauty and elegance. Men's and women's kimonos were distinguished by subtle differences in cut and color. Young women wore brightly colored kimonos with long sleeves, while older women tended to wear shorter sleeves and dress in darker colors.

During the Tokugawa period (seventeenth to nineteenth centuries), the shogunal government tried to restrict expensive and colorful kimonos to members of the samurai class. Merchants and artisans were prohibited from wearing bright colors. The townspeople obeyed this order, outwardly at least, by wearing plain outer garments, but wealthy town dwellers lined these robes with expensive and colorful silks.

After bathing, for sleeping, and for informal wear at home in the summer, men and women wore cotton kimonos called *yukata*.

Peasant Dress

In rural areas, both men and women continued to wear trousers and jackets. Women also wore aprons and head-scarfs. The clothing of peasants was usually made of cotton, dyed dark blue with a dye made from the indigo plant. For women's clothing, the cloth was dyed using a block-printing technique that produced patterns of blue and white.

Shoes

Outdoors, the Japanese wore sandals woven from rice straw. On rainy or muddy days,

Ivory figure of a Japanese peasant woman. Peasants dressed simply, when compared to the wealthier townspeople.

wooden clogs called *geta* were worn instead of sandals. These consisted of a wooden platform fitted on top of two wooden blocks, which raised the foot above the wet ground.

Cosmetics

During the Heian period, cosmetics were worn by both men and women. Under samurai rule, men stopped using make-up, but upper-class women continued to be very fond of cosmetics. Powder was used to whiten the face, rouge was used to color the cheeks and lips, and a vegetable dye was used as nail polish. Women shaved their eyebrows, and used a black powder to paint artificial "moth wing" eyebrows in their place. Clothing was perfumed by holding it over smoking incense burners. Women prided themselves on having very long hair, which was done up in fancy hairstyles decorated with carved, gilded, and jeweled combs. Fans and parasols were carried by both men and women.

Religion and Rituals of the Japanese

Shinto

Shinto, the "way of the gods," was the original religion of Japan. Like many ancient peoples, the early Japanese believed that powerful natural forces that humans could neither explain nor control, such as wind and rain, earthquakes, rivers and mountains, and the heavenly bodies, must be gods that needed to be placated and worshipped. Gods, called *kami,* ranged from minor local deities of mountains, trees, waterfalls, and other natural features, to powerful beings worshipped at great shrines under the protection of the imperial family (which claimed descent from the Sun Goddess).

Natural objects that embodied gods were marked as sacred places by being decorated with a rope made of twisted rice straw. More important sites were given shrines, some small and some very grand, which were entered through sacred gates called *torii*. Large shrines sometimes housed sacred objects, such as mirrors or swords. Such shrines were staffed by priests, musicians and dancers who would perform rituals for people who asked the gods for a good harvest, a wife or a child, or some other favor.

The central belief of Shinto is that gods can be approached only if one is in a state of purity. Illness, a death in the family, and many other things can bring pollution that must be

Sixteenth century Shinto god carved from wood.

This large bronze Great Buddha was built by the Amida Buddhists during the Kamakura period, in A.D. 1252.

cleansed through bathing and rituals before prayers can be offered.

Buddhism

Buddhism, an Indian religion, reached Japan via China and Korea in the sixth century A.D. Buddhism teaches that the inevitable unhappiness of human life is the result of desire. All beings, after death, are reborn in new lives according to the law of **karma,** which says that one's conduct in past lives affects one's happiness in future lives. This cycle of **reincarnation** continues until all desire is overcome, whereupon the enlightened believer becomes a Buddha in an endless state of happiness called **nirvana.**

By the time Buddhism reached Japan, it had developed into many different sects. Originally a simple, monastic religion, it now had great temples with tall **pagodas** and statues of Buddhist deities, complex rituals carried out by priests, and holy scriptures. Most Buddhist sects that became popular in Japan taught that saints, called Bodhisattvas, could aid people in achieving enlightenment.

One of the most important Buddhist sects in Japan was the Pure Land Sect, which placed special emphasis on the Bodhisattva Amida, the Lord of Compassion. It taught that salvation could be achieved by pure faith.

The Lotus Sect was founded in Japan during the Kamakura period by a priest named Nichiren. It taught that the essential teachings of Buddhism were all found in a scripture called the Lotus Sutra.

Zen Buddhism was founded in China, but it became very important in Japan from the Kamakura period onward. Zen teaches that **enlightenment** can be achieved through meditation and intense physical and mental discipline. It became especially popular and influential with members of the samurai class, as well as with artists and intellectuals.

At first Shinto and Buddhism were rivals, but gradually the two religions learned to coexist peacefully. Most Japanese believed in both religions, and worshipped at both shrines and temples.

Important Japanese Rituals and Festivals

Birth

When Japanese women were expecting babies, special prayers were offered for them at both Buddhist temples and Shinto shrines. Pregnant women ate a special diet and wore a cloth waistband that had been blessed at a temple. The act of giving birth was polluting, according to Shinto belief, and the new mother could not enter a shrine until purification rituals had been performed. Both the mother and her house would be purified by being sprinkled with sacred salt. The hearth would be cleaned, and a new fire was then lit.

The birth of a child, and especially of a son, was celebrated with a feast. Births were celebrated in rich and poor families alike.

Detail from a large mural at the Monjudoo Temple, Kyoto, which depicts the soul of a dead person being welcomed into heaven by the Bodhisattva Amida.

Death

A death in the family required that the surviving family members, and the house itself, be purified by Shinto rituals. But the principal ceremonies of death were Buddhist. After a funeral service in the temple, conducted with prayers and chanting, the body was cremated. Ashes were buried in a cemetery beneath wooden or stone tablets offering prayers to the Bodhisattva Amida.

Bon

Bon was a festival with both Buddhist and Shinto elements, celebrated in mid-summer. Then, it was believed, the souls of the dead returned to visit their homes. Cemeteries were tended, dances performed, and paper lanterns and bonfires lit to welcome the souls of the dead, entertain them, and then bid them farewell at the end of the festival.

Shichi-go-san

The children's festival of "seven-five-three" dates from ancient times. Boy and girls three years of age, boys of five, and girls of seven, were taken by their parents to a Shinto shrine to give thanks for having reached these ages safely. The children would be dressed in the finest clothing that their parents could afford.

Obeying the Law

Japan's government was headed by the emperor, whose title was Tenno, "heavenly sovereign." In theory, the emperor was an absolute ruler. In ancient times, Japanese emperors had substantial power, but for most of Japanese history, their power was controlled by other powerful individuals. In the seventh and eighth centuries A.D., emperors tried to establish a Chinese-style system in which the emperor ruled with the aid of a professional bureaucracy, chosen from among the educated elite on the basis of merit. This reflected the Confucian ideal of a society in which there were four classes, as follows:

shi	small educated ruling class
nō	peasants, who were the bulk of the population
kō	artisans who produced goods
shō	merchants who moved things from place to place and made them available for purchase.

At the bottom of the social ladder were other groups, such as criminals, entertainers, and "unclean" butchers and leather-workers.

However, this system of imperial bureaucratic government never became a reality in Japan. During the Heian period, the throne was controlled by the aristocratic Fujiwara family, which made sure that emperors were young, weak, and obedient. From the Kamakura period onward, real power lay with the samurai class, producing this social pyramid:

Samurai or warrior class	
agriculturalists ⎫ artisans ⎬ merchants ⎭	People of these three classes were required to show respect and deference to a samurai. Failure to do so could result in being killed by the offended warrior.

Law

Early Japanese laws dealt largely with such matters as land ownership, and applied to members of the nobility. Commoners had few legal rights, and could be tried for crimes in courts run by aristocratic landlords or their bailiffs. Each family was responsible for the behavior of its members, and most minor civil and criminal cases were settled informally, out of court.

A new code of law adopted in 1721 made justice more uniformly available to commoners, but samurai were still above the law in some respects.

Portrait of Minamoto Yoritomo who became the first shogun in A.D. 1185.

Writing It Down: Recording Things

Until Chinese characters *(kanji)* were introduced to Japan along with Buddhism, Japan had no written language. A few aristocrats and monks learned to read and write in kanji. But Chinese characters, each of which stands for an entire word, are badly suited for writing Japanese, which has a complex grammar quite unlike Chinese. By the ninth century, a phonetic script called *hiragana* was devised (along with a similar system called *katakana);* each symbol represented the sound of a single syllable. This made reading and writing much easier, and literacy became more widespread, among aristocratic women as well as men. Much of the best literature of the Heian period, in the form of poems, diaries, and novels, was written by women.

Eventually most Japanese writing used a hybrid script, with kanji for nouns and verbs, hiragana for modifiers and grammatical particles, and katakana for emphasis.

Calligraphy, the art of writing beautifully, was much admired in Japan. Every well-educated person was expected to practice calligraphy, and a person's handwriting was considered to reveal much about his or her education, social standing, and character. Most Japanese books were printed from woodblock copies of hand-

This scroll is written in a combination of kanji and hiragana script. The illustration is of an archer's equipment.

28

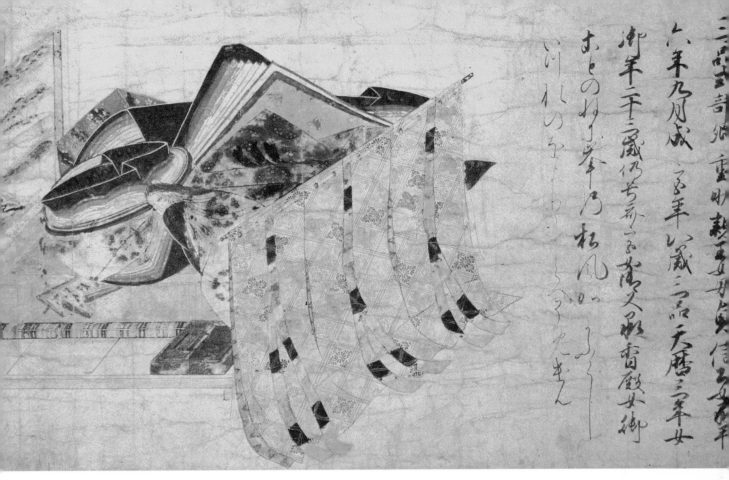

written texts rather than using moveable type, in order to preserve the artistic quality of the writing itself.

Printing

Printing, introduced from China and Korea during the Nara period, was first used to copy Buddhist sacred texts. Later other kinds of literature were printed as well. But poems, stories, letters and diaries continued to circulate in small, hand-copied editions. With the growth of literacy among commoners during the Tokugawa period, printed books became more widespread. The first woodblock-printed newspapers appeared in Japan in the seventeenth century.

Paper

Japanese paper was made from the bark of the mulberry tree. Bark was stripped from branches and boiled with water and ashes to separate the fibers, which were then mixed with water. Screens made of woven split bamboo were dipped into the mixture to produce

Portrait from a scroll painted during the Heian period of the poetess Saigo-no-Nyogo whose poem is inscribed on the scroll. The poem reads, "The breeze rustles the leaves on the hillside and seems to mingle with the tone of the koto. On which string of the koto, I wonder, does the breeze begin to play?". (The koto is a harp-like musical instrument.)

a soft, wet mat of fibers. This was pressed and dried to make a sheet of paper.

Calculating Time

Around 604 A.D. the Japanese adopted the Chinese calendar, which had a solar year of 365¼ days and also a lunar year of twelve 29-day months. Extra months were inserted from time to time to keep the two systems aligned with each other. Peasants also used a folk calendar that relied on natural signs, such as the beginning of the rainy season, and the first frost, to record the passing seasons.

Days were divided into twelve periods, each two hours long. People used sundials to tell the time.

Japanese Legends and Literature

Japanese literature has a long history. The earliest surviving work, written in A.D. 712, is the *Kojiki (Record of Ancient Matters)*. It records the myths, legends, and early history of Japan.

The *Kojiki* also contains the earliest examples of the type of Japanese poetry known as *tanka*. A tanka was composed of five lines and had a set pattern of syllables, 5, 7, 5, 7, and 7 syllables per line, respectively. A collection of tanka called the *Kokinshu (Poems Old and New)* was compiled in A.D. 905. Tanka became very popular during the Heian period. Here is an example from the *Kokinshu:*

Honobono to	My thoughts are with a ship
Akashi no ura no	That slips island hid
Asagiri ni	Dimly, dimly
Shimagakureyuku	Through the morning mist
Fune wo shi zo omou	On Akashi bay

The earliest and greatest collection of poetry, however, was the *Manyoshu (Collection of Ten Thousand Leaves)*, compiled in the eighth century. It contains about 4,500 poems, including some long poems called *choka*.

During the Heian period, formal documents and some Buddhist religious works continued to be written in Chinese, but most literature was written in Japanese, using a combination of kanji and hiragana scripts. Members of the aristocracy, both men and women, frequently wrote poetry and other works of literature.

During the Kamakura period (1185-1333), Japan came to be dominated by the samurai military class. As a result, the literature of the time often featured themes of warfare and glory on the battlefield. The *Heike Monogatari (Tales of Heike)*, a novel about the civil wars of the twelfth century, is the greatest example of this military literature. During this period also, wandering storytellers and Buddhist monks often entertained people with tales of warfare or Buddhist miracle tales. Some of these were later written down.

Haiku

During the Tokugawa period (1600-1867), tanka poetry was given up in favor of the even shorter *haiku* form. The haiku was composed of seventeen syllables in three lines of 5, 7, and 5 syllables, respectively. The essence of haiku lies in its blend of simplicity and subtlety. The greatest master of the haiku form was Matsuo Basho (1644-1694), a former samurai who became a wandering Buddhist monk. Here are two examples of haiku poetry:

Yoshino nite	Come, my old hat—
Sakura misho zo	Let us go and see
Hinoki-gasa	The flowers at Yoshina.
Harusame ya	A spring shower—
Monogatari yuku	While an umbrella and a straw raincoat
Mino to kasa	Pass by chatting.

The Novel

The Japanese novel began during the Heian period, with the writing of *Genji Monogatari (The Tale of Genji)* by Lady Murasaki Shikibu. Written in the early eleventh century, it is about the life and loves of a fictional prince who is portrayed as the ideal aristocrat. This very long book is thought to be the first true novel ever written anywhere in the world. It remains a classic of Japanese literature, and was the model for other Japanese writers of fiction in later periods.

Myths and Legends

The *Kojiki*, and a slightly later work (written in Chinese) called the *Nihon Shoki (Chronicle of Japan)*, contain many myths about the origin of the world, the gods, and the Japanese people. They also record legends about the early rulers of Japan.

The oldest Japanese creation myth tells how the god Izanagi and his sister, the goddess Izanami, crossed a bridge from the heavenly plains to look at the earth, which was covered with water. They stirred the water with a rod, and the first of the Japanese islands appeared. They stepped onto this island, and created mountains, rivers, lakes, and the rest of Japan. Their children also became gods and goddesses. The most important were Amaterasu (the Sun Goddess), Susanowo (the Storm God), and the Moon God.

The Wedded Rocks in Ise Bay are said to have sheltered Izanagi and Izanami. The straw rope which ties the rocks together wards off evil.

Japanese Fairytales

Buddhist monks often told miracle tales and fairytales to teach people about religion. A collection of such stories, *Nihon Reiki (An Account of Miracles in Japan)* was compiled in the ninth century.

One of the most famous Japanese fairytales is *Taketori Monogatari (The Bamboo Cutter's Tale)* which was written in the tenth century. This story tells of a childless man who finds a tiny girl in a bamboo stalk. She eventually grows up and becomes a beautiful woman and many men wish to marry her. As she does not wish to marry, she sets them all impossible tasks with the promise to marry the one who can carry out his task. The emperor himself wishes to marry her but because he is the emperor she does not wish to deceive him in this way. Instead, she dissolves into a ball of light and returns to her old home in the moon.

Art and Architecture

Japanese architecture is well suited to the geology and climate of Japan. Most buildings were made of wood and built with post-and-beam architecture, making them flexible enough to withstand earth tremors. Sliding doors, windows, and interior wall panels made houses cool in Japan's hot, humid summers. However, such houses were vulnerable to fire, and cold in the winter. Few buildings were over two stories in height.

Palaces

Palaces usually had several low buildings connected by walkways and courtyards, covering a wide area. Their architecture was simple but elegant, with clean lines and good proportions. During the Nara and Heian periods, palaces were built in a style based on Chinese public buildings. In later periods, a truly distinctive Japanese palace style evolved.

Castles

Japanese fortified castles were built by feudal lords during the sixteenth and seventeenth centuries. The design of these fortress-palaces included barred windows, gates, trapdoors, and vantage points for firing guns and arrows. Castles were surrounded by high stone walls and moats. The White Heron Castle at Himeji is an outstanding example of castle architecture.

Shinto and Buddhist Architecture

Shinto shrines and Buddhist temples present an interesting contrast in architectural styles. Shrines used a distinctively Japanese style,

The Himeji Castle, also known as the White Heron Castle, was built in 1557, during the civil wars that preceded the Tokugawa period.

while temples were based on Chinese-style architecture.

Shinto Shrines

The design of Shinto shrines is thought to preserve many elements of Japanese architecture from the pre-imperial period. Shrines were simple wooden buildings with thatched roofs, consisting of a single room raised above the ground on stilts and entered by a wooden staircase. The building was surrounded by a wooden wall, and entered through a special gate called a *torii*. Straw ropes hung with strips of white paper marked the shrine as a sacred place, and stone statues of sacred animals were placed in front of it to protect it. Otherwise, the shrine contained no ornamentation, statues, or other decoration.

Shinto shrines were usually located near a sacred rock, tree, or other natural feature, and were surrounded by groves of trees in a setting of great natural beauty. The simplicity and

Sacred stone animals such as this stylized lion were placed in front of Shinto shrines to protect them.

beauty of shrine architecture reflected the Shinto belief in the importance of purity and natural harmony.

Buddhist Temples

Buddhist temples were built in Chinese style. Built of wood on a raised stone platform, they had massive tile roofs held up with thick wooden pillars. In contrast to Shinto shrines, the interior of Buddhist temples contained many statues, paintings, and rich ornamentation. The Horyuji Temple near Nara, built in A.D. 607, is thought to be the oldest wooden building in the world.

Buddhist Influence on Art: Landscaped Gardens

The art of landscape gardening came to Japan from China, along with Chinese-style temple

Japanese landscaped garden with raked sand and pebbles.

and palace architecture. The beauty of gardens and courtyards was as important as the architecture of the buildings themselves.

With the rising influence of Zen Buddhism in the Ashikaga period (1333-1573), garden design reached new heights. Temple gardens were designed to aid monks in meditation, and everything in them had a symbolic nature. Gardens contained ornamental trees such as pines, camelias, flowering plums, and bamboo, as well as areas of white sand raked in ornamental patterns, gnarled volcanic rocks, moss, ponds and lakes, and pathways that led to wooded groves or tea-ceremony pavilions. Gardens were designed to create a feeling of calm and tranquility.

Japanese Flower Arrangement—Ikebana

Ikebana (Japanese flower arranging) was a skilled art, and involved more than just an ability to arrange flowers. As with other art forms influenced by Zen Buddhism, the creation of beauty was considered an aid to re-

ligious enlightenment. The art of flower arrangement originated as early as the Nara period from the custom of offering flowers to statues of the Buddha.

During the Ashikaga period, ikebana developed as one aspect of the tea ceremony, but by the seventeenth century it was recognized as an independent art form. "Flower Masters" taught people how to select flowers and how to arrange them according to strict standards of color, grouping, and line.

Painting

As with many other arts, Japanese painting originally was influenced by Chinese styles, but later developed its own Japanese characteristics. Painting was done on paper or silk, using ink or watercolors. Paintings were mounted as handscrolls, hanging scrolls, or on screens or panels. Subjects included nature paintings, with mountains, trees, flowers, and birds and animals; highly detailed narrative paintings showing scenes of battles, urban life, or court life; and portraits. Zen-style painting specialized in creating images with a few rapid brush strokes, using only black ink.

Lacquerwork

Lacquer is made from the milky sap of the lac tree, to which color (usually red or black) has been added. A base of wood or paper was coated with many layers of this liquid to create a hard, shiny, durable surface that could be decorated with gold leaf or other ornamentation. Introduced from China in the sixth century, lacquerwork became extremely popular in Japan, and Japanese artisans brought lacquerwork to a peak of artistic perfection.

The Japanese used lacquerwork for many items including small cabinets, trays, and cosmetic boxes; bowls and dishes; special utensils for the tea ceremony; and sword scabbards.

Ceramics

Japanese ceramics developed from rough earthenware pottery made for ordinary use by the common people. The techniques of making stoneware and porcelain were introduced from China and Korea. The art of Japanese ceramics was greatly influenced by the tea ceremony. Tea masters placed great value on tea bowls, flower vases, and other objects that reflected the quiet but formal simplicity of the tea ceremony itself.

Metal Casting

The art of bronze casting developed with the spread of Buddhism in Japan. Buddhist temples needed many bronze objects, such as statues, bells, and ornamental metalwork.

Netsuke

During the Tokugawa period (1600-1867), men adopted the habit of wearing small lacquerware cases, similar to purses, suspended by cords from the sashes of their robes. These cases, called *inro*, were held in place by large beads, called *netsuke*, on the cord. Netsuke, made of carved wood or ivory, were miniature works of art, skillfully fashioned in the shape of animals, fruit, or other designs.

Sword Making

Sword making was both a highly skilled craft and an art. In a country dominated by a military aristocracy, swords had to be sharp and strong enough for practical use in warfare, but they were also objects of beauty. Sword blades were fitted with highly decorated hand guards, handles, and scabbards that were made of metal, lacquer, and other expensive materials.

Eighteenth century samurai sword made in imitation of a sword from the Heian period. The sword's scabbard is lacquered and has pearl shell inlay.

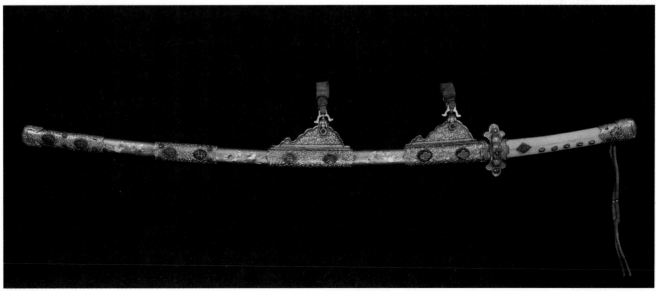

Going Places: Transportation, Exploration, and Communication

Japan's mountainous terrain made transportation and communication difficult for most of its history. Most people lived and died without ever traveling more than a few miles from their place of birth.

Roads

Except near cities and towns, Japan had almost no roads that were suitable for wheeled vehicles. Traffic was limited to people on foot or on horseback, and goods had to be carried by porters or by pack animals. Population centers in valleys or on the narrow coastal plains were relatively isolated from each other.

During the Tokugawa period, the shogunal government maintained a series of highways (really more like footpaths) linking major cities. The most famous of these was the Tokaido Road, which connected the imperial capital of Kyoto with the shogunal capital of Edo (now Tokyo). Inns and wayside rest houses were provided every few miles for travelers on these roads.

1680 map of the Nagasaki port.

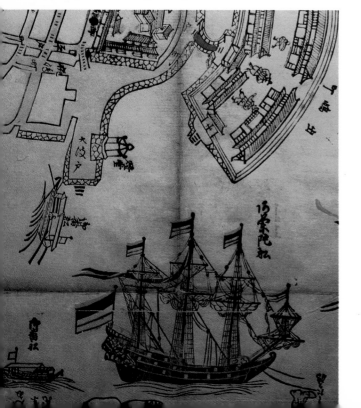

Ships

Japan's rivers are mostly short, shallow, and fast-flowing, making them unsuitable for all but the smallest boats. However, the Inland Sea, which lies between the main islands of Honshu, Shikoku, and Kyushu, provided an artery for sea transportation along coastal areas of western Japan. Fishing boats worked the coastal waters around Japan. Overseas trade with Korea, China, and Southeast Asia was carried out in both Japanese and foreign ships until the seventeenth century, when the shogunal government ordered most foreign trade to cease and prohibited Japanese people from going abroad.

Trade

Ocean trade routes linked Japan to Korea, China, Okinawa, and Southeast Asia from ancient times, but rough seas made this trade dangerous and infrequent. Japan exported lacquerware, sword blades, copper, and sulphur to China and Korea, and imported porcelain, silk, books, and other high-value items. This trade also brought new ideas, inventions, and fashions from the mainland to Japan.

Dangerous seas also made Japan safe from foreign invasion. The Mongols tried twice to invade Japan in the thirteenth century, but both times the invading fleets were destroyed by typhoons.

Portuguese and Spanish ships first reached Japan in the sixteenth century, bringing European goods (including firearms) and Christian missionaries. Fearing the danger of too much foreign influence, the shogunal government expelled most foreigners from Japan early in the seventeenth century. Foreign trade was limited to a few Dutch, Chinese, and Korean merchants at one small trading station at Nagasaki.

Music, Dancing, and Recreation

Music

Japanese musical instruments are mainly derived from instruments introduced from China, Korea, and elsewhere in mainland Asia in ancient times. In Japan, these instruments evolved to take on their own distinctive characteristics. Instruments included drums, vertical and transverse flutes, many kinds of stringed instruments, and cymbals, bells, and gongs. Music was highly valued in Japan not only as an art form, but for its ability to shape and express religious feelings and human emotions. Different instruments were used for different purposes. Sacred dances and Noh drama were accompanied by drums and flutes; Kabuki drama and dances done for entertainment were performed to the music of drums, flutes,

and the *samisen*, a banjo-like instrument with three strings; the *koto*, a large instrument that resembled a harp or a zither, was used for solo musical performances.

Shinto Music

Large Shinto shrines had musicians and dancers who performed as part of religious rituals, to welcome and entertain the gods and seek their help. Village folk festivals also included music and dancing.

Dancing

Dance was an important part of Japanese life. Court ceremonies included formal dances, while at village festivals, the entire population of a village might dance for hours at a time. Types of Japanese dances included:

Musicians performing Gagaku, ancient Japanese court music. Bugaku was the dance form associated with this music, and both became a part of Shinto rites.

Kagura	sacred dances dedicated to gods and performed in villages, courts, and Shinto shrines.
Gigaku	a Buddhist processional dance play using masks carved from wood which were painted and lacquered. Gigaku was brought to Japan from Korea in A.D. 612.
Bugaku	court dances based on Shinto shrine dances, performed by groups of four, six, or eight male dancers. The dances had set movements and patterns. Musical accompaniment included drums, bells, flutes, and panpipes.

Noh

Noh is a distinctive type of Japanese drama that developed during the Ashikaga period from court music and dance of earlier times. Noh is performed on a simple stage with no scenery or props. Actors wear highly expressive masks and elaborate costumes, and perform in a very stylized form of slow dance steps to the music of drums and flutes and the chanting of poetry. Noh plays often are historical dramas that feature not only human characters, but also ghosts, spirits, and demons.

Kabuki

Kabuki is a colorful and very dramatic form of theater which includes both music and dancing. It developed during the Tokugawa period, and appealed to popular urban audiences (in contrast to Noh, which was more of an aristocratic taste). Kabuki plays were often historical dramas or romances with very melodramatic themes. Both male and female roles are played by male actors.

Kabuki is noted for its very elaborate and colorful costumes and facial make-up, and for its contrast between slow, emotional dramatic passages and intervals of fast, vigorous dancing, sword-fighting, and other action scenes.

The eighteenth century is regarded as Japan's golden age of theater. Many of the country's most talented writers wrote plays for Kabuki and Bunraku (puppet theater).

Head of Bunraku puppet representing a young woman from the Tokugawa period.

Bunraku

Bunraku is quite similar to Kabuki, except that it is performed with large hand puppets rather than with human actors. The puppets were manipulated on a small stage by puppeteers who dressed entirely in black to make themselves less noticed by the audience.

Other Recreations

Members of the upper classes were fond of organizing picnics for moon-viewing, cherry-blossom viewing, and other occasions. These group activities were often accompanied by music, poetry recitals, and sake drinking.

Sumo, a kind of wrestling, was originally performed at Shinto shrines, but later became a popular entertainment with professional wrestlers.

Popular sports included shuttlecock (similar to badminton) and a type of football. Several forms of chess were popular among educated people. Members of the samurai class practiced fencing, judo, karate, and other martial arts for sport as well as for military training.

Wars and Battles

During the eleventh century, in the late Heian period, the imperial government of Japan became weaker, and members of the aristocracy attempted to retain their positions of authority with the aid of powerful clan armies. Conflicts led to civil war in the twelfth century, and warriors assumed an important role in Japanese society. With the establishment of military government during the Kamakura period, gentleman-warriors known as samurai ("one who serves") became the dominant force in Japanese government, politics, and society.

The samurai class included powerful feudal lords called *daimyo,* who controlled large armies and ruled their lands almost like independent kingdoms, but also ordinary samurai who were professional warriors who served the daimyo. Members of the samurai class were bound by a code of conduct, called **bushido** ("the way of the warrior"). This code emphasized absolute loyalty to superiors, and a strong sense of personal honor. Samurai would rather die than betray their lords, or suffer the disgrace of being captured in battle. Faced with disgrace, ritual suicide *(seppuku)* was the only honorable alternative.

Originally rough warriors, in later times many samurai became well-educated gentlemen. In peacetime they practiced Zen meditation and cultivated such arts as the tea ceremony, flower arranging, and calligraphy.

Dress of the Samurai

In peacetime the samurai adopted the ordinary dress of the upper classes, a silk kimono of the finest quality, color, and pattern. They shaved their heads high above the forehead, and wore the back of their hair long and tied up in a distinctive knot. Outside their own homes, samurai wore a pair of long swords at all times.

In battle, the samurai wore armor made of small steel scales laced together with silk cords. This armor protected the upper body and shoulders, and had skirt-like panels to protect the lower body. Arm guards, heavy gloves, and shin and thigh guards were also worn. The face was protected by a steel mask, and a heavy helmet with hanging panels of scale armor was worn to guard the head and neck.

This battle armor was quite striking and colorful. It was lacquered in bright colors and held together with colored silk cords. Helmets

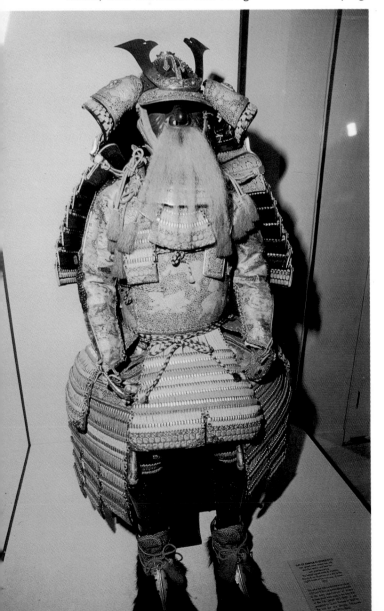

Twelfth century armor of a samurai. The helmet has horns, and the mask was designed to be terrifying.

were often decorated with horns or other ornaments, and face masks were designed to look like a human face contorted with ferocious rage.

Detail from a sixteenth century screen painting depicting an armorer at work. The various pieces of the samurai's armor are fashioned by the craftsmen and apprentices.

Swords and Guns

The two-handed samurai sword was the supreme weapon of war in Japan. Swords were treated with reverence and respect, and were considered sacred to Hachiman, the God of War. Swordmakers were highly honored. From the Kamakura period onward, the ownership and use of swords was restricted to members of the samurai class. Samurai warriors trained for hours each day from early childhood to learn to become skillful swordsmen. Samurai also learned to fight with bows and arrows, spears, and daggers, and were also trained in unarmed combat.

Firearms were introduced into Japan by Portuguese merchants in 1541. They were quickly adopted by rival daimyo for use in the civil wars of the sixteenth century, and many swordsmiths turned their skills to producing copies of these new weapons. By 1560 great feudal lords were able to field armies of thousands of foot soldiers armed with muskets. Guns presented a great threat to the power of the samurai class, because a common soldier with a gun could easily kill a samurai despite his armor, swords, and long years of military training. With the unification of Japan by the Tokugawa shogunate in 1600, strict laws were passed to restrict the production and ownership of guns, and limit their use in battle. Thus the power of the sword-wielding samurai class was preserved for another two and a half centuries, until the coming of modern warfare in the mid-nineteenth century.

Japanese Inventions and Special Skills

Woodblock Printing

Printing was invented in China in the seventh century A.D., and soon was adopted in Japan. Wooden blocks were carved in reverse with words or pictures, inked, and used to print on a sheet of paper. Moveable type was also invented in China several centuries later, but was seldom used in Japan. Because of the importance of beautiful calligraphy in Japan, and the complexity of the kanji, hiragana, and katakana written scripts, most books continued to be block printed.

In the seventeenth century, Japanese artists began to use the woodblock printing technique to produce colored pictures. A separate block was carved for each of the colors used, and the blocks were printed onto a sheet of paper one by one to build up the colored image. In the hands of such artists as Utamaro, Hiroshige, and Hokusai, these colored block prints reached a high artistic standard. Prints depicting famous places, Kabuki actors, female entertainers, and other subjects were sold in shops and became very popular with townspeople during the Tokugawa period.

Textile Arts

Since ancient times, members of the upper classes in Japan were fond of dressing in clothing made from highly colorful and elaborate silk textiles. As a result, dyers and weavers in Japan developed a wide variety of techniques for producing beautiful textiles to satisfy this market. Many different styles of weaving were employed, as well as embroidery, tie-dyeing, and block-print dyeing to decorate the cloth.

Even ordinary articles used by peasants and other commoners were often made of beautiful textiles. Printed or tie-dyed blue and white cotton was used for cushion and mattress covers, curtains, wrapping cloths, as well as cloth for clothing.

The Tea Ceremony (Cha-no-yu)

The tea ceremony, which achieved the status of a living art form during the sixteenth and seventeenth centuries, also served to stimulate other arts to a high peak of perfection. Tea masters insisted on the best of everything for the setting and the utensils of the tea ceremony. Architects, garden designers, and masters of flower arranging were challenged to create the most beautiful possible settings for the tea ceremony. Lacquer workers, metal workers, potters, and other artisans put forth their best efforts to produce kettles, tea bowls, serving utensils, vases and other tea ceremony articles. Because it unites so many different arts, the tea ceremony is often regarded as the most important of all Japanese arts.

Miniaturization

The Japanese excelled at the art of finely detailed decoration of many objects for daily use. Fans, *inro, netsuke,* and other personal objects were treated as tiny works of art. Houses might have tiny interior landscaped gardens of only a few square feet in area. Perhaps the peak of miniature arts in Japan was the creation of *bonsai,* trees that were carefully shaped and tended in pots and allowed to reach a maximum growth, after many years, of only a foot or two. Like many other Japanese arts, the technique of creating bonsai originated in China but was perfected in Japan.

Why the Civilization Declined

Throughout history, the Japanese adopted many ideas, arts, and techniques from foreign countries and gave them a distinctive Japanese character. Japan's entry into the modern era in the late nineteenth century was a continuation of this process; traditional Japanese civilization did not "decline" so much as it was transformed by the adoption of new ideas.

Europeans first reached Japan in the sixteenth century, bringing with them firearms, Christianity, and many new ideas about science, medicine, and philosophy. At first the Japanese government welcomed, or at least tolerated, foreigners. But by the early seventeenth century the Tokugawa shogunate worried that Christianity and other foreign ideas might undermine their government. As a result, Christians were persecuted and almost all foreigners were expelled. The only Europeans in Japan were a few Dutch traders at Nagasaki, who were allowed to remain not only because

of the value of foreign trade, but because they provided news of the outside world.

Japan succeeded in maintaining its isolation from the rest of the world until the mid-nineteenth century. In 1853-1854 an American naval officer, Commodore Matthew Perry, arrived in Japan, demanding that Japan open its doors to free foreign trade. The Tokugawa government, unable to oppose Perry's heavily armed ships, agreed to his demands. But many young samurai were outraged by the government's weakness. They rebelled, and in 1867 ousted the last shogun and restored imperial rule under the young emperor Meiji.

Japan's new leaders quickly realized that Japan would only be able to stand up to the Western world if it entered the modern age. Japan began to build railroads, steamships, and factories, and introduced universal education and constitutional government.

Instead of becoming "Westernized", Japan took many things from the West and made them Japanese in order to transform Japan into a powerful, modern nation.

Detail from a sixteenth century screen showing Portuguese traders and Jesuit missionaries bathing.

Glossary

Archaeologists People who study cultures, especially prehistoric cultures, by examining artifacts that are excavated, and dating them.

Anthropologists People who study the dynamics of human cultures.

Artisans Craftspeople who create or produce hand-made goods such as pottery, textiles, lacquer, or metal-work.

Bailiff In Japan, a land agent or estate manager who supervised peasant farmers and collected land rents on behalf of an absent landowner.

Bodhisattva An enlightened person who delays entry to Nirvana, so as to come back to earth to help others attain enlightenment.

Brazier A metal or ceramic receptacle for holding burning charcoal or other fuel; used for heating rooms.

Bushido The name given to the samurai code of honor. The name means "the way of the warrior".

Concubines Secondary wives who lived in a man's house without being legally married to him.

Emperor The Japanese emperor in theory ruled over the whole country in the same manner as the emperor of China. At the same time he was the traditional high priest who made peace with the gods for the benefit of his people. Emperors often had little real power. From 1185 to 1867, the government was completely controlled by shoguns, or military rulers.

Enlightenment In Buddhism, the state of freedom from all desire, which allows one to escape from the cycle of reincarnation governed by karma.

Feudalism A political system in which a ruler exercises power through noblemen who govern their own territories but are personally loyal to him. In Japan, feudal lords were members of the samurai class. Peasants were not free to leave their lands, and had to pay high rents to the feudal lord.

Karma A Buddhist belief that a person's status in life has been determined by his or her deeds in a previous life or incarnation, and that one's actions in this life determine one's status in the next life.

Nirvana In Buddhism, the eternal state of release, attained through enlightenment, from the cycle of reincarnation governed by the laws of karma.

Paddy field A field in which rice is grown. It can be flooded when the rice is planted, and drained for the harvest.

Pagoda Buildings that were a part of Buddhist temples. They were towers reaching up to twelve stories, with each storie diminishing in size, with a mast at the top ringed with metal discs.

Reincarnation A Buddhist belief that the soul, upon death of the body, is reborn in another body or form.

Sake A type of wine brewed from rice. Sake was usually heated before serving.

Samurai One of the Japanese warrior caste that became particularly powerful after the eleventh century. The name Samurai means "one who serves".

Shogun In Japan, the head of a military government and leader of the samurai class. From 1185 to 1867, the government of Japan was controlled by shoguns, supposedly on behalf of emperors but really in usurpation of their power.

The Japanese: Some Famous People and Places

JIMMU TENNO

Jimmu Tenno is regarded as the first emperor of Japan, and the founder of the imperial family that still sits on the Japanese throne. Almost nothing is known for certain about him, however, and the only sources of information are myths and legends recorded in early books like the *Kojiki* and the *Nihon Shoki*. The dates traditionally ascribed to him, in the seventh century B.C., are too early by at least three hundred years. In myth, Jimmu Tenno was a descendant of the Sun Goddess Amaterasu through her grandson Ninigi, whom she sent to govern the earth and who married a grandchild of the storm god, Susanowo.

In 1890, a Shinto shrine was erected at the supposed site of Jimmu Tenno's burial place at Unebi.

EMPRESS SUIKO TENNO

Suiko Tenno was the first woman in recorded history to reign as ruler of Japan. She was the daughter of Emperor Kimmei, and the wife of Emperor Bidatsu, who reigned from A.D. 572 to 585. Bidatsu was succeeded as emperor by Yomei, who died soon afterwards. Feuding broke out among three powerful families, the Soga, Mononobe, and the Nakatomi. The Soga clan won the struggle, and supported Emperor Sushun, who gained the throne. He was murdered in 592, and his younger sister Suiko became the ruler.

Buddhism became established in Japan during Suiko's reign, and many aspects of Chinese culture were introduced.

PRINCE SHOTOKU TAISHI

Shotoku Taishi was an influential prince and intellectual who lived from A.D. 573 to 620. The second son of Emperor Yomei, he was a member by marriage of the powerful Soga clan. He became the leading figure in the government during the reign of Empress Suiko Tenno.

Shotoku Taishi sponsored trips by envoys to China, who brought back new ideas when they returned to Japan. He promoted Buddhism and Confucianism, and strengthened the power of the Japanese throne by adopting Chinese-style political institutions, thus protecting the imperial family from the rivalry of great aristocratic families. In 604 he wrote the "Seventeen Article Constitution," based on Chinese political ideas, which called for loyalty to the throne and for respect for Buddhism and Confucianism.

Under Shotoku Taishi's leadership, Japan adopted the Chinese calendar. He was also responsible for improvements in public works, such as roads and irrigation systems. His most lasting legacy, however, was the building of Buddhist temples. He was the founder of the Horyuji Temple, built near Nara in 604; the buildings of the Horyuji are now the oldest wooden buildings in the world. After his death, Prince Shotoku came to be regarded as a Buddhist saint.

NARA

Nara was the first permanent capital city in Japan, and served as the nation's capital from 710 to 784. It was laid out in the style of a Chinese capital city, with a grid pattern of large and small streets; unlike a Chinese city, however, it had no city wall because Japan's emperors had no fear of being attacked by enemy armies.

During the eighth century, when Nara was the capital, a great many Buddhist temples were built there. Nara's many temples soon became very wealthy and powerful, one reason why the capital was moved to Heian-kyo after only seventy-five years. Housed in one of Nara's temples is the Nara Daibutsu (Great Buddha), the largest bronze statue in the world.

Also in Nara is the Kasuga Taisha, or Grand Shrine of Kasuga, one of the oldest Shinto shrines in Japan and the family shrine of the Fujiwara clan. Its garden paths are lined with over 3,000 stone lanterns.

HEIAN

Heian-kyo, the Capital of Tranquility and Peace, became Japan's capital city in 795. Sometimes called simply Kyoto ("capital city"), it remained the imperial capital until 1869, when the imperial throne was moved to Tokyo. Like Nara, Heian-kyo was laid out in a grid pattern, without a city wall. The city was located on both banks of the Kamo River in a valley between two small mountain ranges.

From the time of its founding until the outbreak of civil war in the twelfth century that led to the establishment of shogunal rule, Heian-kyo was dominated by a brilliant aristocratic society centered around the imperial court. During the Heian period, Japan was peaceful and wealthy, and literature, art, music, and the decorative arts flourished.

FUJIWARA FAMILY

The Fujiwaras were one of the most remarkable families in Japanese history. Throughout the Heian period, from 795 to 1185, they dominated the imperial government and were the leaders of aristocratic society.

The family was founded by Nakatomi Kamatari (614-669). As a reward for protecting the heir to the throne in a time of clan warfare, the emperor gave him a new surname, Fujiwara. His descendants cultivated a special relationship with the imperial family; the empress was almost always a daughter of the Fujiwara family. Emperors were encouraged to retire to Buddhist monasteries at a young age, leaving real power in the hands of the head of the Fujiwara clan. As a result of this special position, the family acquired great power and wealth, and controlled large amounts of land.

After the establishment of shogunal rule in 1185 the Fujiwaras lost much of their wealth, but they continued to hold a leading position among the old Kyoto aristocracy.

SESSHU

Sesshu was a leading artist during the Ashikaga period, and one of Japan's greatest masters of ink painting (sumi-e). From the age of ten, he was educated in calligraphy, painting, and religion at a Zen temple. He moved to Kyoto in about 1440, where he studied under a famous artist named Shubun. Twenty years later, he became the chief priest of a Zen temple at Yamaguchi. After about 1466, he used the pen name Sesshu (Snowy Boat). In 1468 he went to China, where he studied religion and painting at Buddhist temples and was held in high esteem by the Chinese people.

After Sesshu returned to Japan in 1469 he painted his greatest masterpieces, using a combination of Chinese and Japanese techniques and ideas. His paintings include landscapes, religious themes, and screen paintings of birds, flowers, and plants.

TOKUGAWA FAMILY

The Tokugawa family controlled the government of Japan from 1600 to 1867, when imperial rule was restored. The family was descended from a son of the Emperor Seiwa, who ruled during the ninth century. In 1600, at the Battle of Sekigahara, Tokugawa Ieyasu defeated his main rival, Toyotomi Hideyoshi, and brought about the reunification of Japan after decades of civil war.

Tokugawa Ieyasu moved the shogunal government from Kyoto to Edo (now Tokyo) in 1603. He and his successors closed Japan to most outsiders, and prohibited Christianity. Cut off from the rest of the world, Japan during the Tokugawa period enjoyed a long period of peace and prosperity. Cities grew larger, and a rich merchant class grew up in the cities and towns. Feudal government was closely regulated, with all daimyo required to show obedience to the shogun.

Fifteen shoguns of the Tokugawa family ruled Japan for over two and a half centuries before the last one, Tokugawa Keiki, was deposed by the Meiji Restoration in 1867.

Index